Original title:
Labyrinth of the Eternal Heart

Author: Kaido Väinamäe
ISBN HARDBACK: 978-1-80561-457-9
ISBN PAPERBACK: 978-1-80561-482-1

Frolicking in the Fields of Longing

In the fields where daisies sway,
Children laugh and dance away.
Whispers of the cool, sweet breeze,
Encircle hearts with gentle ease.

Underneath the vast, blue sky,
Dreams take flight, they soar and fly.
Chasing butterflies at play,
Living in the light of day.

Golden hours, soft and warm,
Nature's beauty, pure and calm.
Every moment, joy bestowed,
In this place where love has flowed.

Yet within, a yearning grows,
For the past that no one knows.
Beneath the laughter, shadows creep,
In the heart where secrets sleep.

Frolicking with hope in hand,
Together, we will surely stand.
In the fields, we find our way,
Chasing dreams that never fray.

Gates of Perpetual Affection

In twilight's glow, where shadows blend,
Hearts whisper secrets, dreams ascend.
A bond unbreakable, firm and true,
Through storms we wander, me and you.

With every breath, a promise made,
In love's embrace, we shan't degrade.
The world may turn, but here we stand,
Soul to soul, hand in hand.

Within the Veil of Hidden Yearnings

Behind closed eyes, desires creep,
Silent wishes, buried deep.
Stars align in the quiet night,
Guiding dreams to take their flight.

Every heartbeat, a tender plea,
Seeking solace, yearning to be free.
In shadows cast by fleeting grace,
I find your essence, a warm embrace.

The Maze Where Echoes Reside

Winding paths of silent cries,
Lost in thoughts that never die.
Each echo whispers tales untold,
In this maze, our hearts unfold.

Through winding turns and dusky ways,
Hope flickers softly, ablaze.
Every corner holds a sigh,
Reminding us of times gone by.

Paths Woven from Hope's Fabric

Threads of dreams stitched with care,
Creating paths, vital and rare.
We walk together, step by step,
With every stride, a vow adept.

A tapestry of light and shade,
Every moment lovingly laid.
Through hope's embrace, we find our way,
Turning night into bright day.

Echoing Steps in the Realm of Affection

In quiet woods where whispers blend,
Soft echoes call, as heartbeats send.
Each step we take, a newfound grace,
In this warm realm, we find our place.

Beneath the boughs, where shadows play,
Light dances softly, guiding our way.
We speak in looks, the world fades out,
In gentle silence, love sings loud.

The rustling leaves, a sweet embrace,
Every sigh, our secret space.
A melody of hearts in tune,
As stars awaken, night meets noon.

With every breath, the moments bloom,
In tangled roots, we dispel gloom.
Our laughter weaves through time and air,
In this affection, nothing compares.

So let us wander, hand in hand,
Through every heartbeat, understand.
In echoing steps, love finds a home,
In this vast realm, together we'll roam.

The Infinite Dance of Love's Pursuit

In twilight's glow, we spin and sway,
Two souls entwined, dusk turns to gray.
With every glance, a spark ignites,
In this dance of heart's delights.

The music swells, we lose our fears,
As laughter flows, and joy appears.
With gentle steps, we break the night,
In shadows deep, we find our light.

Around we twirl, the world dissolved,
In rhythms sweet, our hearts resolved.
Through every turn, the pulse aligns,
In every whisper, love defines.

The stars above bear witness true,
To every promise made anew.
In this embrace, we lose the chase,
And find our home in love's warm space.

So let us dance, without a care,
In endless nights, a love to share.
With every beat, we find our part,
In infinite steps, we guard the heart.

Crossing the Threshold of Enchanted Affection

At dusk, the portal softly glows,
With every step, our garden grows.
An arch of dreams, we dare to climb,
Hand in hand, we touch the sublime.

Through fragrant paths where echoes dwell,
In whispered spells, our hearts propel.
Each threshold crossed, a secret shared,
In layers of love, we're both ensnared.

The stars ignite in twilight's hush,
With each embrace, the worlds all rush.
In this enchanted, timeless flight,
Our spirits soar into the night.

Through silver streams, our laughter flows,
In love's pure light, each moment bestows.
With eyes that gleam like morning dew,
We cross together, past the view.

Let us tread where few have been,
In realms of magic, love's sweet sheen.
With every blush, affection reveals,
In this enchanted space, love heals.

In the Depths of Desire, We Find Our Way

In shadows deep, where secrets lie,
Desire blooms, like fireflies.
With whispered dreams, our souls ignite,
In searching depths, we find the light.

The heart's fierce call, a siren's song,
In tangled paths, we both belong.
Through longing's ache and sweet embrace,
In this vast sea, we find our place.

With every breath, a promise grows,
In silent nights, our passion flows.
In fervent heat, the world dissolves,
In depths of yearning, love evolves.

We weave our stories, thread of fate,
In the quiet hush, we eagerly wait.
With tender glances that say more,
In such desire, our spirits soar.

So let us dive into this dance,
In the depths where love's advanced.
With open hearts, we'll find our way,
Through shadows deep, love's light will stay.

Threads of Fortune in the Tangle

In shadows where the whispers cling,
Fortunes twist, and secrets sing.
Each thread a tale, a woven fate,
Entwined in hope, yet sealed by hate.

The fabric frays, the colors clash,
As dreams dissolve in silent flash.
Yet in this tangle, light may gleam,
A silver thread within the dream.

With every knot, a lesson learned,
From burning bridges, hearts are burned.
But threaded paths can still unite,
A tapestry, in dark or light.

So hold your threads with gentle care,
Let not despair consume the air.
For in the weave, a story's spun,
In tangled fates, we're not yet done.

The Hidden Gates of True Affection

Behind the walls where shadows play,
Lie hidden paths to light the way.
With gentle hands, we seek the door,
To find affection evermore.

A key of trust, it fits just right,
Unlocking hearts with tender light.
In whispered tones, our secrets bloom,
Dispelling doubt, dispelling gloom.

Through tangled vines, we stumble blind,
Yet love will seek and surely find.
In every glance, a silent plea,
To enter through this gate, set free.

The hidden gates stand firm and tall,
Inviting souls to rise or fall.
With every turn, a chance to grow,
In true affection's sacred glow.

Exiles in the Maze of Emotion

We wander lost in winding paths,
Through labyrinths of joy and wrath.
Each corner turned, a choice to make,
In turbulent seas, our hearts may break.

Exiles tread with weary feet,
In search of solace, hope, and sweet.
But every twist reveals the cost,
Of what is gained, and what is lost.

The walls of doubt, they rise and loom,
Yet flickers guide us through the gloom.
In tangled feelings, truth will shine,
As we embrace the ties divine.

Through tears and laughter, we will find,
The paths that bind both heart and mind.
In this maze where echoes call,
We search for love, the greatest hall.

The Core of Unbroken Currents

Beneath the surface, rivers flow,
Unseen forces, deep and low.
In currents strong, we find our base,
A pulse of life, an endless grace.

With every wave that crashes near,
The core remains, we hold it dear.
Through storms that test, we stand our ground,
For in this heart, true strength is found.

Electric threads that bind and weave,
A tapestry of love, believe.
Through tides that rise and waters churn,
The core of us will always burn.

So anchor deep in trust's embrace,
For in this dance, we find our place.
In unbroken currents, we shall thrive,
Together, always, we are alive.

The Hidden Map of Connected Souls

In shadows deep, our paths align,
A whispered bond, so rare, divine.
With every glance, a truth unfurls,
Λ hidden map of two lost worlds.

Each heartbeat speaks, a silent song,
In unison we find we belong.
With every touch, a spark ignites,
Unraveling stars on endless nights.

Through tangled trails and whispered dreams,
We navigate life's flowing streams.
In every tear, a lesson learned,
In every joy, the fire burned.

The compass true, it points to you,
In this vast sea, a love so true.
A journey shared, we brave the storm,
In the hidden map, our hearts keep warm.

In twilight's glow, our stories meet,
Two wandering souls, forever sweet.
The world may fade, but we will shine,
In the hidden map, your heart is mine.

The Tides of Unseen Heartstrings

Beneath the surface, rhythms flow,
A silent dance, a soft hello.
Through waves of time, we press, we pull,
The tides of souls, so deep, so full.

With every rise, a swell of dreams,
In gentle whispers, the moonlight beams.
The ocean's breath, it calls our names,
In secret currents, we ignite flames.

The heartstrings tug, a hidden plea,
In ocean depths, you're calling me.
We'll weave our fates through sea and sky,
On tides of love, we dare to fly.

In crashing waves, our shadows blend,
With every wave, love has no end.
From shore to shore, we sail away,
On tides unseen, our hearts will stay.

With every night, the stars will guide,
In this vast sea, there's no divide.
While silver tides may shift and curl,
In unseen heartstrings, love's a whirl.

Secrets Beneath the Surface of Desire

In quiet whispers, dreams reside,
Beneath the waves, where hopes confide.
A depth unknown, a longing bright,
Secrets stored in the cloak of night.

With each soft sigh, a tale unfolds,
In every glance, a world beholds.
The spark of love, so sweet, so pure,
In hidden depths, we yearn for more.

The surface glimmers, yet hides the truth,
Desires tangled in our youth.
With every heartbeat, shadows play,
Unveiling dreams in a dance of sway.

In moonlit paths, we chase the light,
Unraveling fates in the velvet night.
Every secret, a treasure vast,
In the tapestry of the future's cast.

So take my hand, together we'll roam,
Through desires, we'll find our home.
For beneath the surface, we both dare,
To seek the secrets lying bare.

The Ensnared Pulse of Connectivity

In tangled webs, our souls entwine,
A pulse that beats in sacred line.
Through every glitch, the sparks ignite,
In unseen ways, we feel the light.

A dance of shadows, we intertwine,
In silent chords, our hearts align.
With every laugh, a vibrant thread,
In this embrace, our spirits spread.

The gentle hum, the unspoken tie,
In every glance, the heartbeats fly.
Through all that binds, we find our way,
In the ensnared pulse, we choose to stay.

The world outside may seem so vast,
But here we dwell, forever cast.
A symphony of souls combined,
In perfect tune, our hearts designed.

So let us weave this tale anew,
In pulses shared, our love rings true.
For every moment that we find,
In connectivity, our hearts are blind.

The Heart's Uncharted Territory

In shadows deep, the heart explores,
Whispers of dreams behind closed doors.
With every beat, a secret found,
In silence where the lost are bound.

A compass made of hopes and fears,
Guiding through the vale of tears.
Each path diverges, twists, and turns,
In every flame, a longing burns.

New wonders call, the spirit flies,
Beneath the vast and endless skies.
With courage drawn from depths unseen,
The heart unveils what might have been.

Through wild terrain and fickle breeze,
Emotions weave like whispered trees.
In every glance, a map unfolds,
The heart's uncharted tales retold.

To venture forth, to seek, to find,
In love's embrace, the heart aligned.
In wonders lost, in truths profound,
The heart's uncharted ground unbound.

Whispers Beneath the Vines of Time

Amid the vines, old secrets sway,
Where echoes of the past still play.
In tender notes, the stories grow,
With every twist, new paths bestow.

Beneath the leaves, the whispers sigh,
In every breath, the days gone by.
The dance of fate through tangled roots,
In fading light, we find our truths.

As seasons change, the tales remain,
In every heart, the threaded chain.
Connected souls across the years,
In silent bonds, we share our fears.

The vines entwined, a tapestry,
Woven with love, our history.
In moments past, we plant the seeds,
Of dreams we grow, the heart still leads.

Beneath the stars, the future calls,
In whispered hopes, the spirit stalls.
Through time's embrace, we dare to climb,
To find our place 'neath vines of time.

Sentinels at the Crossroads of Longing

In twilight's glow, the watchers stand,
Guardians of dreams, hand in hand.
With every choice, a path unwinds,
In longings deep, our fate defines.

Beneath the weight of night's soft hue,
The echoes call, the heart breaks through.
Divided roads with signs obscure,
In silent whispers, we endure.

Each step we take, a promise made,
In shadows cast, we won't evade.
Through crossroads fraught with hope and doubt,
The sentinels keep watch throughout.

With every tear, a lesson learned,
In moments lost, our spirits yearned.
The heart, it knows, though paths may part,
The journey lives within the heart.

With courage bright, we search the skies,
Where futures shine and pasts arise.
At crossroads' end, our souls align,
In tender grace, love seeks to find.

An Odyssey Through the Heart's Labyrinthine

In winding ways, the heartbeat flows,
Through labyrinthine paths it goes.
Each twist and turn, a fate to weave,
In every pause, we learn to believe.

The walls adorned with dreams once known,
In every corner, seeds have grown.
Through echoes soft of love's refrain,
The heart's own odyssey of pain.

A journey long, yet filled with grace,
In shadows deep, we find our place.
As love unfurls, a guiding light,
Through every maze, the heart takes flight.

With open minds, we dare to roam,
In every heartbeat, we find home.
Through trials faced and pathways crossed,
The heart embraces all that's lost.

One step anew, one breath divine,
In every choice, our dreams align.
Through each refrain, our spirits sing,
An odyssey, the heart's own wing.

Heartstrings Entwined in Cosmic Patterns

In the night's embrace, we dance slow,
Stars above us twinkle and glow.
Hands entwined, a celestial bind,
Whispers of love in the infinite mind.

A universe spun with threads of gold,
Every moment, a story told.
Galaxies swirl in the depths of our eyes,
Boundless and bright as the endless skies.

Time stretches out in a velvet caress,
Each heartbeat echoes, a lover's confess.
In shadows we roam, hand in hand,
Finding our place in this vast, grand land.

Together we weave through the endless space,
Creating a bond time cannot erase.
With every star that we reach to claim,
Our heartstrings flourish, forever the same.

So here's to the ties that the cosmos spun,
A journey together, two souls as one.
In the tapestry bright of the night sky,
We'll etch our love until the stars die.

The Spiral of Longing and Belonging

A winding path through dream's embrace,
Echoed footsteps in a sacred place.
Yearning hearts that twist and turn,
In this spiral of love, we learn.

With every breath, we draw in tight,
Searching for warmth in the frigid night.
In every glance, a promise beams,
Woven together in fragile dreams.

Like the tides that ebb to the shore,
We find ourselves longing for more.
In the depths of our souls, a flame ignites,
Illuminating paths in the darkest nights.

Through the twist of fate, we fight and strive,
In this dance of longing, we come alive.
Together we rise, together we fall,
In the spiral of love, we heed the call.

So take my hand, let's embrace this ride,
In the warmth of your heart, I will abide.
Amidst swirling chaos, we will find a song,
In the spiral of longing, where we belong.

In the Heart's Depths, We Wander

In the quiet depths of the heart's dark cave,
Whispers of memories that long to be saved.
Footsteps echo in the silence profound,
Where secrets and shadows alike are found.

We tread softly on the paths of regret,
Where love once bloomed, but now we forget.
Yet sunrise brings a new light in view,
Each dawn a canvas, painted anew.

Along these corridors, we softly roam,
Finding treasures where the heart calls home.
Fragments of laughter, the warmth of a smile,
We capture these moments for just a while.

In this sacred space, we uncover our scars,
And learn to embrace the light of the stars.
Together we navigate the labyrinth's twist,
In the heart's depths, we find what we've missed.

So let us wander through this sacred hall,
Where echoes of love in our spirits enthrall.
Hand in hand, let's explore every part,
In the heart's depths, we forever start.

A Tapestry of Unfading Memories

Threads of gold and silver shine bright,
Weaving together in gentle light.
Each moment a stitch in the fabric we spin,
A tapestry filled with where we've been.

Laughter and tears, they intertwine,
The colors of life in a grand design.
In this rich canvas, our stories we tell,
Of joy and heartache, of heaven and hell.

With each passing season, the patterns will grow,
Memories cherished like flowers in snow.
We gather the fragments of days gone by,
Making a quilt that wraps and won't die.

Through time's gentle hands, we'll carry the weight,
Of moments that taught us to love and create.
In the fabric of life, we find our place,
A tapestry woven with love and grace.

So here's to the memories, bright and alive,
In the tapestry of hearts, we deeply thrive.
Forever entwined in this intricate weave,
A story of love that we'll never leave.

The Solitary Journey of the Affected Heart

In silence whispers of the night,
I wander through the shadows bright.
Each star a tear, each moon a sigh,
As echoes fade, I ask them why.

The road is long, with bends and curves,
Each memory like a jagged nerve.
Yet onward moves this heavy soul,
In search of peace, in search of whole.

Footsteps linger on the ground,
In solitude, no voice is found.
With every step, the heart does ache,
A fragile trust, a fragile break.

I carry dreams both bright and dim,
A song of hope to buoy the grim.
Through storms and trials, I shall tread,
In search of love, not fear or dread.

And though the path ahead is stark,
My heart echoes its hopeful spark.
For every journey that I take,
Might lead to joy, or hearts that break.

Threads that Bind in the Depths of Feeling

In woven strands, our hearts entwine,
A tapestry of love divine.
Through laughter shared and sorrows cried,
The bonds of life we won't divide.

Each thread a memory softly sewn,
In vibrant hues, our truth is shown.
With every stitch, a story told,
In colors warm and threads of gold.

Yet shadows loom, they weave their own,
In depths of feeling, seeds are sown.
Through trials thick and trials thin,
We find the strength to grow within.

The fabric of our souls does blend,
In gentle arcs that never end.
Each heartbeat echoes in this art,
As life's great dance moves from the heart.

Together we rise, together we fall,
These threads of feeling bind us all.
For in this life, through all we do,
The depths we share define us true.

A Tapestry Woven with Heartstrings

In gentle weaves of vibrant strands,
A tapestry of dreams expands.
Each heartstring pulled, a note of song,
Together weaves where we belong.

With colors bright and shadows deep,
The fabric draws and gently keeps.
A story spun in every hue,
Reflects the love we cling to true.

Though threads may fray and edges wear,
The woven cloth reveals our care.
In every tear, a lesson learned,
With every stitch, our passion burned.

From whispers soft to echoes loud,
Each moment shared, we stand so proud.
A quilt of life, a patchwork whole,
In tangled threads, we find our soul.

Together through all storms we fight,
Our tapestry shines, adorned with light.
For in each heartstring, love does cling,
A beautiful song, eternally sing.

The Overgrown Path of Broken Promises

Upon this path, the weeds have grown,
Each promise made, now overthrown.
The echoes of the words we said,
Reside in shadows, lost and dead.

With every step, the thorns do bite,
A journey steeped in loss and plight.
The memories haunt like ghosts at night,
In silent whispers, wrongs must right.

Yet down this road, I still must tread,
To find the truth that's loosely spread.
For even broken dreams can shine,
In pieces scattered, hearts align.

The light breaks through the darkened trees,
In every crack, a slight reprieve.
And though the path is rough and long,
A spark remains, a fading song.

Through brush and bramble, I will roam,
To claim my heart, to find my home.
For on the overgrown, I see,
The strength it takes to truly be.

Forks in the Road of Affection

Two paths lay ahead of me,
One warm, the other cold,
Love's whispers guide my feet,
But which story will unfold?

In shadows, truths collide,
Doubt dances in the night,
Yet courage sparks a flame,
Illuminating the right.

With every step I take,
The heart sways like a tree,
Listening to its own rhythm,
Setting my spirit free.

Fingers brush through tender air,
Promises shimmer in the light,
Forks in the road are many,
Only one leads to delight.

As choices shape the journey,
I savor every chance,
For love's true destination,
Is found in each sweet glance.

Through the Thicket of Memory

In silence, memories bloom,
Whispers of days gone by,
Through dense thickets of time,
I seek the reasons why.

Footprints in the soft earth,
Mark the paths I dare tread,
Glimmers of laughter echo,
In the spaces where I've fled.

Each hidden corner beckons,
With secrets wrapped in thread,
Love's tapestry unfolds,
In hues of joy and dread.

Through tangled vines of longing,
I stumble and I find,
The shadows of my heartbeats,
Pulse within my mind.

Emerging from the thicket,
With stories carved in gold,
The past weaves through the present,
Yet its embrace is bold.

Fables Carved in the Soul's Mist

In whispers soft as dawn,
Fables call from the haze,
Each tale a glimmering thread,
In the fabric of our days.

Carved upon the heart's stone,
Lies the echo of a dish,
Crafted from life's longings,
In the soft, elusive mist.

Characters dance in shadows,
Stories linger in the air,
Love and loss intertwine,
Secrets laid bare with care.

Fables spark the spirit,
Awakening dreams untold,
In the realm of the soul's mist,
Timeless truths unfold.

We find strength in the legends,
Writing our own paths bright,
For in each fading fable,
We gather love's pure light.

The Enchanted Walkways of Desire

Underneath the moon's gaze,
Desire's steps intertwine,
Along paths of soft whispers,
Hearts rhythmically align.

Through gardens lush and green,
Every bloom tells a tale,
Of passion gently weaving,
In the fragrant evening veil.

Footfalls on the cobblestones,
Echo love's sweet refrain,
As shadows dance in twilight,
Both pleasure and the pain.

With each turn and corner,
New dreams unfold like a rose,
In the enchantment of the night,
Where fervent longing grows.

The walkways beckon softly,
With mysteries to explore,
In the heart's enchanted garden,
Desire forever soars.

The Quest for Hidden Hearts

In the forest of dreams we tread,
Whispers of secrets softly spread.
Through thickets of memory we roam,
Searching for places that feel like home.

Each path a chance to find our way,
As sunlight begins to break the gray.
With every step, the heartbeats rise,
Unmasking truths behind the skies.

Lost in the echoes of laughter bright,
We chase the shadows, embrace the light.
In corners hallowed with timeless grace,
Hidden hearts reveal their space.

The quest, a journey to feel alive,
Within the chaos, our spirits strive.
Together we learn to face the day,
Finding love's treasures in disarray.

Amidst the thorns and tangled vines,
We gather the moments, the sacred signs.
In the quest for hidden hearts, we heal,
Unraveling layers, revealing what's real.

The Shadows Where Love Lurks

Beneath the stars, whispers arise,
In quiet corners, where passion lies.
The shadows dance with a tender grace,
Holding secrets in a soft embrace.

In the twilight, silhouettes play,
Love lingers where the light fades away.
Hidden glances and quiet sighs,
Fragrant whispers where longing cries.

Every heartbeat echoes the night,
Chasing dreams in a world of light.
Together we wander, lost in the dark,
Writing our story with a spark.

Through narrow alleys where no one goes,
Love finds its way where the wild rose grows.
In shadows deep, we dare to explore,
The quiet corners, forevermore.

With every turn, a glimmer appears,
In the shadows where love disappears.
We find our way, hand in hand,
In the depths of night, we understand.

Beyond the Walls of Silent Grief

In the hush of moments lost in time,
A heart once full now struggles to climb.
Beyond the walls where silence dwells,
Echoes linger, weaving their spells.

Each tear a tale, a river of pain,
Flowing gently through love's dark lane.
We carry the weight of dreams long gone,
Yet hope still flickers like the dawn.

Among the ruins of what we knew,
We search for signs, for life anew.
Through cracks in stone, a light breaks through,
Guiding us forward, with courage true.

In gardens where memories softly bloom,
We plant the seeds that conquer doom.
In silence, we learn to speak again,
Finding the strength to dance in the rain.

Beyond the walls, there's love to find,
A gentle promise, tender and kind.
In the echoes of grief, we forge our way,
Turning shadows into a brand-new day.

The Circles We Draw in Time

With every heartbeat, we trace a line,
In circles, we dance, through love's design.
Moments entwined, like threads of gold,
Stories of warmth that never grow old.

In the laughter shared, we draw our fate,
A tapestry woven, intricate and great.
Through trials faced and secrets kept,
The circles we draw are never inept.

Time spins a web, delicate and fine,
In each loop and curve, our spirits align.
We gather at crossroads, where paths collide,
Finding the strength to walk side by side.

Through seasons of change, we learn and grow,
In circles we find the love we know.
Each heartbeat a rhythm, each sigh a rhyme,
Embracing the journey, the circles of time.

As we circle back to where we began,
We cherish the moments, hand in hand.
In the circles we draw, we find our place,
A never-ending dance, a warm embrace.

Through the Echoes of Faded Glories

Amidst the dust of ancient days,
We find the signs of lost praise.
Faded glories whisper low,
In shadows where the wild winds blow.

Time holds tales of love and pain,
Echoes dance like summer rain.
Forgotten dreams that once took flight,
Now linger softly in the night.

Memory's song, a haunting tune,
Plays beneath the watchful moon.
As stars reflect the paths we chose,
In twilight's glow, the past still flows.

With each heartbeat, echoes share,
The stories woven through the air.
Resonating in the silent space,
Where faded glories find their place.

We walk the lines of time's embrace,
Through corridors that memory trace.
Together we weave what's left behind,
In echoes sweet, our souls aligned.

The Landscape of Lonesome Echoes

In valleys deep, where shadows sigh,
Lonesome echoes drift and fly.
The breeze carries tales of yore,
Through landscapes where voices implore.

Mountains rise like dreams untold,
Guarding secrets, brave and bold.
In twilight's glow, the silence reigns,
While lonesome hearts bear hidden pains.

Footsteps linger in the mist,
Whispers of love that we can't resist.
The landscape speaks in muted tones,
To the restless souls who roam alone.

Crisp leaves tumble, truth laid bare,
In the cool and crisp autumn air.
Every echo, a story spun,
Of laughter lost, of battles won.

So let us wander, hand in hand,
Through this lonesome echoing land.
For in each sound, a memory gleams,
And love once lost, is still in dreams.

Weaving Through the Fabric of Love's Labors

In fields where golden wildflowers grow,
We weave the threads of love's soft glow.
Each strand a story gently spun,
In the tapestry of two as one.

With hands entwined, we twist and turn,
As flames of passion brightly burn.
The fabric stretches, shimmers bright,
In every stitch, our hearts ignite.

Through trials faced and joys we share,
We craft a world beyond compare.
A labyrinth of dreams and care,
Each knot a bond, each tear laid bare.

From laughter's thread to sorrow's seam,
We stitch together every dream.
In this creation, fierce and true,
The fabric whispers, "I love you."

Together woven, we stand strong,
With every heartbeat, every song.
In love's embrace, we find our way,
As we weave onward day by day.

The Unseen Threads of Affection

In quiet corners of the heart,
Unseen threads begin to start.
A gentle pull, a silent call,
Binding souls with love's soft thrall.

Across the miles, connections made,
Invisible paths where dreams cascade.
Each thought a bond, a whispered breeze,
In the stillness, our spirits seize.

Through laughter shared and tears we've shed,
In every moment, love is fed.
These threads, though hidden from our sight,
Weave a pattern, pure and bright.

With every glance, our gazes meet,
The unseen threads, a bittersweet.
In secret places, love does bloom,
A melody that chases gloom.

So let us cherish these soft ties,
For true affection never dies.
In the fabric of life's embrace,
The unseen threads will find their place.

Celestial Spheres of Intertwined Souls

In twilight's glow, we drift and dance,
Our spirits weave in cosmic chance.
The stars align, a silent tune,
As dreams take flight beneath the moon.

In whispered winds, our secrets blend,
A tapestry of souls, transcend.
Through galaxies, our hearts will roam,
Together, find a cosmic home.

In silence deep, we cast our gaze,
To boundless night, our souls ablaze.
Each heartbeat syncs with starlit song,
Intertwined, where we belong.

With every breath, the universe sways,
As light and dark embrace the rays.
Through nebulae, our love will soar,
In endless realms, forevermore.

So let us wander, hand in hand,
Across the skies, through time we'll stand.
In celestial spheres, we'll intertwine,
A love eternal, pure, divine.

A Sanctuary of Echoing Dreams

In whispered halls of velvet night,
Our dreams unfold, a soft delight.
Echoes linger in the air,
As visions dance with gentle care.

A sanctuary, where hearts can soar,
Through secret doors, we ask for more.
With every sigh, a wish takes flight,
In this embrace of purest light.

The shadows twine, they seem to weave,
A tapestry of hope we believe.
In every corner, memories bloom,
Our laughter fills the silent room.

Outside the world may swirl and spin,
But here, our journey does begin.
A tranquil place, our souls align,
In echoing dreams, forever shine.

So close your eyes and drift away,
In this haven, here we'll stay.
With every heartbeat, we will find,
A sanctuary for the mind.

Footprints on the Sands of Forever

On golden shores, where tides embrace,
Footprints mark our secret place.
With every step, the waves recede,
A dance of love, a timeless creed.

The sun dips low, the sky ignites,
Painting paths of amber light.
In every grain, our stories track,
Memories etched, no turning back.

With gentle whispers, the oceans call,
Each moment shared, we risk it all.
Together we carve our wild array,
In this realm where dreams won't fray.

As dusk descends, the stars appear,
A guiding light to quell our fear.
Footprints washed by waves' embrace,
In the sands of forever, we trace.

Through fleeting time, we leave our sign,
In every sunset, love divine.
Our journey lingers, come what may,
Forever held, in ocean's sway.

The Compass of Unrequited Passions

In shadows deep, desires bloom,
A heart that aches, wrapped in gloom.
Each glance unshared, a silent plea,
A compass lost, with no decree.

Through tangled thoughts, our paths diverge,
A gentle spark, yet just a surge.
In every sigh, unspoken words,
The song of love that goes unheard.

With hopes alight, we chase the dawn,
But winds of change keep pulling on.
A bittersweet dance of give and take,
In dreams, my heart you softly break.

Yet still I hold this flame so bright,
Through endless days and lonely nights.
The compass spins, its needle sways,
Leading to you, in twisted ways.

With every heartbeat, still I yearn,
For moments shared, when tides may turn.
In unrequited, I stand tall,
A lover's heart, despite it all.

The Circular Dance of Boundless Hearts

In twilight's glow, two spirits meet,
With every step, their souls entreat.
Around they twist, in joy they spring,
A symphony of love takes wing.

With laughter bright, they soar the skies,
In every glance, the promise lies.
Their hearts entwined, forever bold,
A timeless tale that won't grow old.

Through moonlit nights and dawn's embrace,
They find their strength in shared space.
In turn and spin, they lose all fears,
Together woven through the years.

With every beat, a rhythm found,
In unity, their hearts resound.
A dance that circles, never ends,
In boundless love, their spirit bends.

Unraveling the Layers of Devotion

Beneath the skin, a story lies,
Each layer peeled, the truth defies.
With tender touch, the heart unfolds,
In whispered trust, a warmth it holds.

Time weaves a tapestry so fine,
With threads of love that intertwine.
In quiet moments, layers blend,
Revealing depths that never end.

Lost in the echo of shared breaths,
They chase the shadows, face their deaths.
In vulnerability, strength is born,
A bond forever, never torn.

Through storms and trials, hand in hand,
A shelter built upon the sand.
With every heartbeat, layers twine,
In devotion's glow, their hearts align.

Fragments of Forever Lost

Scattered dreams, like autumn leaves,
Echoes of laughter, soft reprieves.
In whispered sighs, the past remains,
Fragments of love in silent chains.

Through broken glass, reflections stare,
Moments frozen in the air.
Each shard a tale of what once was,
In aching hearts, the memory buzz.

With every pulse, they sift the dust,
Searching for pieces, clinging to trust.
In shadows cast, they find the light,
A flicker of hope in the endless night.

Yet in the ruins, beauty thrives,
In fractured paths, a spark arrives.
From fragments lost, new worlds emerge,
In every loss, the heart will surge.

The Serpentine Road to Connection

Winding paths beneath the trees,
Whispers drifting in the breeze.
Each twist and turn, a lesson learned,
In every heart, a fire burned.

With every step, the world expands,
A dance of fate, entwined hands.
Through valleys deep and mountains high,
They chase the stars, they touch the sky.

In tangled roots, foundations grow,
Deep in the soil, their feelings flow.
Through winding roads, new horizons seek,
In connection's arms, they find the peak.

The road may bend, yet hearts will stay,
In unity, they find their way.
Through serpentine paths, they navigate,
In love's embrace, they celebrate.

Tangles of Time and Sorrow

In shadows cast by memories lost,
The clock ticks on, but at what cost?
Each moment tangled, threads entwined,
A tapestry of dreams maligned.

Through whispered winds and fading light,
We search for clarity in the night.
Yet sorrow sows its binding thread,
In every tear, a story bled.

Yet hope blooms in the darkest hour,
A fragile heart, a fledgling flower.
We gather strength from pain once known,
In tangled roots, we find our own.

The passage swift, the seasons change,
Yet still we long, we rearrange.
For in the chaos, love shall rise,
A beacon bright beneath the skies.

As time unravels, we embrace,
The scars, the laughter, every trace.
For in our hearts, the journey winds,
To treasure all that life unwinds.

The Unraveling of Love's Enigma

In tender whispers, secrets flow,
A riddle wrapped in hearts aglow.
We seek the truth in every glance,
Yet love remains a daring dance.

Through tangled thoughts, the embers spark,
As shadows blend within the dark.
Each heartbeat echoes, soft and sweet,
A puzzle woven, bittersweet.

With every kiss, a piece reveals,
The skin remembers how it feels.
In passion's storm, we lose our way,
Yet in the chaos, we shall stay.

The questions linger, answers hide,
Yet in our souls, love's tide will glide.
For in the depth of deep despair,
The enigma breathes, a lover's prayer.

As two collide, a flame ignites,
In trembling hands, the world alights.
With every tear, a lesson learned,
In love's embrace, our hearts discern.

Secrets Between the Heartbeats

In the silence where shadows dwell,
Lies a story we dare not tell.
Between each breath, a longing sigh,
A secret whispered, never shy.

The world spins round, a carousel,
Yet here we stand, our hearts compel.
In fleeting moments, eyes will meet,
An unspoken bond, bittersweet.

For in the pause between the noise,
Our souls converse, in timeless poise.
The rhythm soft, a tender beat,
As two become one, incomplete.

Through every glance, we share our fears,
In quietude, we shed our tears.
A sanctuary, where we find,
The secrets held entwined in mind.

Forever sheltered, ever near,
In heartbeats' dance, we disappear.
Each pulse a chapter, pen in hand,
We write our love, a story planned.

The Chasm of Unseen Connections

Between the stars, a silence swells,
Where unseen ties weave tales and spells.
A chasm deep, yet hearts will bridge,
In flickering sparks, we dare to ridge.

With every breath, a bond unwinds,
In secret places, love defines.
Through empty spaces, echoes call,
Reminding us we're not so small.

The world expands, yet draws us close,
In quiet moments, love engrossed.
Each whisper shared, a thread of gold,
In timeless dance, our story told.

Though distance parts what hearts may hold,
Connections flourish, bright and bold.
In every glance, a universe,
Where unseen ties our souls converse.

Together, we traverse the night,
In shadows' embrace, we find the light.
For in the chasm, love will reign,
An unseen force, our sweet refrain.

Riddles of the Endless Yearn

Whispers dance in twilight's glow,
Secrets trapped in time's soft flow.
Hearts beat loud, yet voices small,
In silence deep, we hear the call.

Questions linger in the dark,
Flickering like a dying spark.
What lies beyond the veils we chase?
Riddles weave in a haunting space.

Every sigh a cautious play,
Yearning for a brighter day.
Lost within this endless maze,
Searching for forgotten praise.

Dreams like rivers twist and turn,
Through the shadows, we all yearn.
With each tear, a lesson learned,
In the void, our souls have burned.

Yet hope remains, a fragile thread,
Through tangled paths, it softly led.
Together, we will find the air,
In riddles of the endless yearn.

Threads of Infinity's Embrace

In the loom of time, we weave,
Threads of dreams we dare believe.
Colors blend in cosmic dance,
Life unfolds in a timeless trance.

Stitch by stitch, we build our fate,
Every moment, we create.
Whispers of the stars above,
Wrap us tight in threads of love.

Tangled paths and winding ways,
Guide us through the longest days.
In the shadows, light will trace,
Threads of infinity's embrace.

Galaxies twirl in the mind,
Echoing the ties that bind.
With each heartbeat, we will soar,
Forever seeking something more.

Fractals of our history,
In every stitch, a mystery.
Through the fabric, hope will shine,
Threads of time, forever twine.

Journey Through the Twisted Ways

Hold my hand as we embark,
Through twisted paths, we face the dark.
Every turn, a tale untold,
Guided by the brave and bold.

In the labyrinth, shadows creep,
Secrets buried, dreams to keep.
With each step, a heartbeat blends,
On this journey, time transcends.

Footprints faded in the dust,
Trust the road, it's a must.
Navigating the quiet maze,
Journey through the twisted ways.

Stars above us paint the night,
Calling forth the inner light.
In the chaos, echoes roam,
Every corner leads us home.

Tales of courage linger near,
In the silence, we can hear.
As we wander side by side,
Hearts united, hearts our guide.

Shadows of Unfulfilled Dreams

In the shadows, dreams reside,
Hopes once high, now set aside.
Echoes whisper from the past,
Lessons learned but never grasped.

Flickering flames of what could be,
Wander through this memory.
Fractured wishes floating high,
Like the fading twilight sky.

Every heartbeat tells a tale,
Winds of change, a ghostly sail.
In the darkness, we reclaim,
Shadows of our lost acclaim.

Yet in this hush, a spark ignites,
Hope takes flight on fragile nights.
Emerging from the silent screams,
We rise up, despite the dreams.

With the dawn, new paths unfold,
Bold adventures to behold.
In the light, we'll find our gleam,
Casting off our shadows' scheme.

Veiled Passages of the Soul

In shadows deep, the silence dwells,
Whispers echo, casting spells.
Veiled truths behind closed doors,
Searching heart, always explores.

Time will stretch, a fragile thread,
Paths unwound where few have tread.
In depths of night, the soul will sing,
A melancholic offering.

Secrets held with tender care,
In twilight's hush, we lay bare.
The dance of thoughts, a fleeting spark,
Guides us through the endless dark.

With every step, the past may fade,
Yet echoes linger, memories made.
Each moment shared, a soft refrain,
Binding us with joy and pain.

A veiled passage to the light,
With every turn, we chase the night.
The soul's own map, forever drawn,
In the depths, a new dawn.

Bonds Forged in the Fire of Twisting Paths

Through winding roads, we wander still,
In the warmth of passion, hearts will thrill.
Together we face the storms that roar,
Bonds forged in fire, we become evermore.

Every trial, a test we embrace,
In the heat of struggle, we find our place.
The flames of fate may scorch and bite,
Yet we rise stronger, igniting the night.

In twisting paths, our spirits unite,
Drawing strength from the darkest plight.
Hand in hand, we climb the heights,
Guided by love, our burning lights.

With laughter shared and tears we shed,
The bonds we forge will never fade.
For in the fire, our souls are trained,
In each heart's armor, passion is gained.

No distance can sever what we've built,
Through every layer, love's thread is spilt.
In the annals of time, our story will last,
Bonds forged in fire, forever steadfast.

The Secret Language of Heartbeats

In quiet moments, whispers bloom,
Heartbeats echo in the room.
A rhythm speaks where words may stall,
In the ballet of silence, we hear it all.

Each pulse a story, softly penned,
A language spoken, hearts will send.
Connected deeply, we dance and sway,
In the secret code, come what may.

In the stillness, our souls align,
Unraveled secrets, pure and divine.
With every thump, the world fades away,
Wrapped in the warmth where love will stay.

A tapestry woven of dreams and sighs,
With each heartbeat, the universe replies.
In every throb, a promise made,
In this sacred space, fears will fade.

Listen closely, the heart will teach,
In its gentle pulse, love's lesson's reached.
The secret language, timeless and true,
In every heartbeat, I find you.

Labors of Love in the Twilight

In dusk's embrace, we toil and mend,
The chores of love, where paths do blend.
With gentle hands, we craft our care,
Labors of love, a bond we share.

Each tender gesture, as stars ignite,
Illuminating tasks through the night.
In every moment, the heart's soft plea,
A testament of love, wild and free.

Among the shadows, dreams unfold,
Stories whispered in the twilight gold.
We build our world with patient grace,
In this sacred labor, we find our place.

With every stroke, our souls align,
In the weave of life, love's design.
Through sweat and laughter, we rise above,
Harvesting joy in the fields of love.

In twilight's glow, we cast our nets,
Harvesting sunsets, no regrets.
For in each labor, a promise is spun,
Love's sacred work, never done.

A Heart's Journey Through Time's Snare

In shadows deep, where echoes play,
A heart beats soft, then drifts away.
Through whispered sighs and muted cries,
It wanders forth, 'neath vastening skies.

Time weaves its thread, a fragile line,
Moments linger, yet swiftly entwine.
Each pulse recalls a distant dream,
As memories shimmer, like starlit gleam.

The sun will rise, a guiding flame,
Illuminating paths that bear its name.
With every step, the past will bleed,
But forward still, the heart must lead.

In twilight's glow, the journey bends,
Where joy and sorrow twist as friends.
For every tear, a lesson learned,
In embers of love, the soul is burned.

Thus journey on, oh heart so bold,
Through tempests wild and nights so cold.
For in the snare of time's embrace,
You'll find the truth, your finest grace.

Wanders of the Veiled Conscience

In the depths where shadows wane,
A whisper stirs amidst the pain.
Veil lifted softly, secrets soar,
Through corridors of mind, explore.

Echoes dance in fractured light,
Guiding thoughts to take their flight.
A quest within, where doubts reside,
In hidden depths, the truths abide.

Each winding turn leads to a choice,
Among the silence, hear the voice.
To face the fears, the heart must dare,
In search of wisdom, rich and rare.

Shattered mirrors, pieces gleam,
Reflections form, a tangled dream.
Wanders deep through veils we weave,
In realms where only few believe.

For on this path, a treasure lies,
In every tear, in every sigh.
To know oneself, the greatest find,
In wanders of the veiled mind.

The Winding Way of Acheron

Upon the banks of shadowed streams,
Pathways twist, like faded dreams.
Here whispers echo, lost in verse,
As souls embark, through fate's cruel curse.

The river flows, both dark and deep,
Where secrets rest and silence keeps.
Each step unfolds a tale untold,
In depths of night, where hearts grow cold.

Phantoms guide with gentle hands,
Through tangled roots and shifting sands.
Yet light may flicker, hope remains,
In winding ways, through joys and pains.

For every turn leads to the heart,
Where sorrows blend with love's sweet art.
Acheron sings its haunting tune,
As stars above begin to swoon.

So journey forth, brave traveler bold,
Beyond the dark, where warmth unfolds.
In winding paths, you'll find your way,
Through Acheron's soft, tender sway.

Guardians of the Forgotten Desires

In quiet realms where wishes fade,
Guardians stand, their vows displayed.
Each silent whisper, each echoed plea,
A testament of what shall be.

Forgotten dreams lay buried deep,
In shadows where the lost ones weep.
Yet softly glows a gentle flame,
To stoke the heart, to call the name.

From ashes rise the hopes once scorned,
In light of dawn, new lives are born.
A tender hand, a knowing glance,
Awakens souls to dare and dance.

Guardians watch the fleeting hours,
As seasons bless with fragrant flowers.
They hold the keys to all we crave,
In hidden paths, the brave may save.

For in their care, we will find grace,
Restoring dreams to rightful place.
With every wish the heart inspired,
The guardians keep our souls desired.

Veils of Mystery in a Heartfelt Quest

Beneath the stars, a whisper sighs,
Shadows dance in the midnight skies.
Veils of mystery softly unfold,
Stories of journeys yet to be told.

In the quiet, secrets reside,
Echoes linger where dreams collide.
Hearts wander in the moon's embrace,
Seeking truths in a timeless space.

Through foggy paths, we choose our way,
Guided by hope, we greet the day.
Each step a note in life's sweet song,
We find where our spirits belong.

Questions rise like mist at dawn,
In search of love, we carry on.
With every breath, we weave our fate,
In the quest for peace, we shall not wait.

Underneath it all, we stay true,
Veils of mystery hide me and you.
Every heartbeat, a sign, a clue,
In the heartfelt quest, we'll follow through.

Hidden Corners of the Soul's Reverie

In quiet alcoves, thoughts take flight,
Whispers echo in the soft twilight.
Hidden corners twist and entwine,
Dreams awaken, like vintage wine.

With each moment, memories bloom,
Softly illuminating the darkened room.
Souls unravel in tender hues,
Finding solace in the shared muse.

Beyond the surface, layers peel,
Unearthing truths we long conceal.
Hearts collide in a dance of fate,
In our reverie, we learn to wait.

Voices linger in shadows cast,
Echoes of futures and whispers of past.
In this realm, connections thrive,
Driving the pulse that keeps us alive.

In hidden corners, we ask why,
Underneath the vast, starlit sky.
In the soul's reverie, we explore,
Together we seek, forevermore.

A Map of Feelings Yet to Explore

Across the landscape of heart's desire,
Lies a map where passions conspire.
Paths yet drawn with ink of dreams,
Each journey flows like river streams.

In the valleys of joy and pain,
Every terrain holds wisdom gained.
Mountains high, where hopes ascend,
A cartographer of love, we send.

Winds of change whisper with grace,
Guiding us to a sacred place.
With every turn, new visions rise,
Hidden treasures beneath the skies.

Through forests deep, we wander still,
Each heartbeat echoes a gentle thrill.
With every feeling, a landmark found,
In the quest for joy, we are unbound.

So let us journey, hand in hand,
A map of feelings, vast, unplanned.
In the endless search, we implore,
The beauty of love yet to explore.

The Corridor of Unspoken Bonds

In the silence where souls align,
Whispers linger, soft as wine.
A corridor stretches, dimly lit,
Unspoken bonds in shadows sit.

Eyes meet briefly, stories unfold,
In the quiet, emotions bold.
Threads of connection gently tie,
A tapestry woven, no need to try.

Each heartbeat echoes, a subtle call,
In the space between, we stand tall.
With every glance, the truth conveys,
In silent moments, love displays.

As we wander through time and space,
Seeking solace in each embrace.
In every pause, a world unknown,
The corridor calls us, we have grown.

In unspoken bonds, our voices blend,
Together we walk, around each bend.
In this silence, our hearts respond,
Forever cherished, the mystery fond.

Mysteries of the Soul's Intertwined Journey

In twilight's grasp, shadows blend,
Time weaves tales, where dreams extend.
A dance of thoughts in silent flight,
Whispers of stars guide the night.

In corridors of heart's desire,
Voices mingle, sparks of fire.
Through winding paths, two hearts will trace,
The essence of love in a timeless space.

Each beat a secret, soft and light,
Fleeting moments, pure delight.
An echo deep within the core,
A journey's bond, forevermore.

With every breath, a story starts,
Intertwined like woven arts.
Through trials, joys, and endless dreams,
The path unfolds in silver streams.

Together they rise, together they fall,
In the labyrinth of the soul's call.
Velvet skies hold their wishes true,
In mysteries shared, just they two.

A Maze of Whispered Secrets

Among the shadows, secrets lie,
In whispers soft, where echoes sigh.
A maze of thoughts, through paths unseen,
Draped in silence, a world serene.

Echoing tales of hearts entwined,
With every turn, a truth defined.
In corridors where hopes collide,
Secrets bloom, and fears subside.

Fragrant memories in the air,
Moments shared, a tender flair.
Behind each door, a story waits,
The mystery of love dictates.

Through winding halls, we soar and sway,
Guided by dreams that light the way.
In questions asked, the answers hold,
The courage found in hearts so bold.

Embrace the stillness, lose the chase,
In whispered paths, we find our grace.
The maze will lead to love's bright heart,
Where every secret plays a part.

Pathways of Unending Desire

Beneath the moon's soft silken glow,
Pathways stretch where wishes flow.
In every step, a fire ignites,
Desire's dance in starry nights.

With every heartbeat, dreams will rise,
Carved in sighs beneath the skies.
Through tangled woods and streams so clear,
The call of longing draws us near.

In the stillness, shadows play,
Guiding souls along the way.
With every glance, every touch,
The essence of love means so much.

Fates entwined in a cosmic thread,
In fleeting moments, words unsaid.
The yearning deep, the hunger wide,
In pathways where our hearts abide.

In the echoes of our souls' refrain,
We'll lose ourselves, we'll break the chain.
Together in this sweet embrace,
Unending desire, time can't erase.

Echoes in the Hall of Longing

In ancient halls where echoes call,
Soft whispers linger, memories fall.
Each corner turned, a story shared,
Resonant sighs, hearts bared.

Through arches wide, the shadows creep,
In every chamber, promises keep.
Longing dances in the dim-lit glow,
Footsteps tracing paths we know.

Reflections of love on cold stone walls,
The pulse of time in gentle thralls.
Lost in thought, we wander through,
In the gallery of dreams, I find you.

A tapestry woven in threads of gold,
In every echo, a truth untold.
Desire lingers in the air,
A symphony of hearts laid bare.

In this hall of yearning's embrace,
We learn the steps, we find our place.
Together we walk, through shadows long,
Echoes of love, where we belong.

Whispers in the Endless Maze

In the silence, voices dance,
Lost in shadows, fleeting glance.
Winding pathways, secrets veiled,
Every turn, a story hailed.

Footsteps echo, soft and light,
Chasing dreams into the night.
Muffled whispers, guiding thread,
Leading hearts where fears have fled.

Walls of ivy, thick and tall,
Breathe the stories of them all.
Unraveled thoughts in tangled air,
In this maze, we wander bare.

Solitude wraps like a cloak,
In every moment, words unspoke.
Yet the light upon us glows,
In the maze, our spirit knows.

Through the labyrinth, hope will soar,
In the whispers, we find more.
Endless echoes, soft and sweet,
In this maze, our souls will meet.

Echoes of an Infinite Love

In the dawn's soft, golden light,
Hearts collide and take to flight.
Unseen ties that gently bind,
In this love, we seek and find.

Every heartbeat sings our song,
Melodies where we belong.
In the silence, shadows play,
Echoes whisper, here I'll stay.

Through the valleys, over hills,
In our laughter, time stands still.
Moments captured, pure and true,
In each other, we renew.

Sailing seas of endless time,
In your eyes, I see the rhyme.
Carved in stars above so bright,
Infinite love, our guiding light.

As the moon ascends the skies,
In this dance, our spirits rise.
Through the ages, hand in hand,
In love's echo, we'll withstand.

The Twisting Path of Desire

A flicker in the midnight air,
Draws us close, a whispered dare.
In the shadows, passions burn,
Through the night, we twist and turn.

Fingers trace on skin so warm,
Wrapped in feelings, safe from harm.
Every glance, a spark ignites,
As we dance through endless nights.

Hearts entwined in fervent spree,
Chasing dreams, wild and free.
Winding roads that never cease,
In this desire, we find peace.

Secrets linger in the dark,
With each touch, we leave a mark.
In the stillness, breaths align,
In the path, our souls entwine.

Desire's twist, a thrilling chase,
Every moment, time we brace.
In this journey, hearts conspire,
Through the twists, we rise higher.

Shadows in the Hall of Yearning

Flickering lights, a haunting tune,
Shadows creeping, soft as June.
In the hall where dreams reside,
Longing whispers, hopes denied.

Every corner holds a tale,
In their silence, voices pale.
Footsteps echo, lost in thought,
In the shadows, love is sought.

Moments linger, time stands still,
Treading softly, hearts will thrill.
In the dark, a warmth we share,
In this hall, we shed our care.

Glimmers of light, a spark ignites,
Through the shadows, love takes flight.
In this yearning, dreams arise,
Chasing hopes beneath the skies.

With open arms, we face the night,
In the hall, our souls delight.
Yearning shadows, infinite lore,
In this space, we ask for more.

Secrets Woven in Time's Embrace

In shadows deep, whispers reside,
Where dreams and silence softly collide.
Moments captured, a fragile thread,
Carried forward, where heart's been led.

Golden hours, lost yet found,
In echoes of love, we are unbound.
Holding tightly what time can't sever,
Secrets woven, now and forever.

Through seasons' turn, we walk the line,
Holding hands, your heart in mine.
With every breath, a promise made,
In this embrace, we'll never fade.

Memories dance, in twilight's glow,
Paths interlace, as rivers flow.
Time a guardian, a gentle guide,
In its arms, we choose to bide.

These secrets kept, for eyes that see,
The timeless love, just you and me.
In every heartbeat, a story told,
Woven in time, both brave and bold.

The Enchanted Tangle of Affection

Amidst the vines where laughter grows,
In tangled smiles, affection flows.
A glance, a touch, a fleeting spark,
In shadows bright, we leave our mark.

Gathering blooms from paths we tread,
With petals soft, where dreams are spread.
In every heartbeat, a whisper sweet,
Two souls entwined, no chance of defeat.

Through moonlit nights, our spirits soar,
In tangled destinies, forevermore.
With every journey, hand in hand,
In enchanted realms, our love does stand.

Beneath the stars, we weave our tale,
In every breath, where love prevails.
Bound by yearning, we dance and spin,
In a vibrant world, where all begin.

Softly we drift, on waves of light,
In the tapestry woven, hearts ignite.
The enchanted tangle, a beautiful sight,
In the arms of love, we take flight.

Threads of Passion in a Timeless Web

In twilight's glow, our passions rise,
In every glance, a world of sighs.
Threads delicate, yet tightly spun,
In this timeless web, we are one.

Under the stars, our hands entwined,
In whispered secrets, hearts aligned.
Crafting moments, each one a gem,
Through life's fabric, a vibrant hem.

With every heartbeat, a story flows,
In passion's flame, our love still grows.
Threads of courage, woven tight,
In daylight's warmth, and the cool of night.

Bearing witness to the truth we seek,
In silent talks, we softly speak.
The dance of time, a gentle sway,
Within this web, forever stay.

With laughter shared, and tears that bind,
In this vast tapestry, love defined.
Threads of passion, forever bright,
In a timeless weave, our spirits ignite.

A Journey Through Endless Emotion

In the realms of heart, we begin to roam,
A journey unfolds, leading us home.
With every tear, and every smile,
Through endless emotion, we walk each mile.

From dawn's first light to twilight's fade,
We share the dreams, we are not afraid.
In waves of joy and tides of pain,
Through stormy skies, our love does reign.

With every heartbeat, we chase the dawn,
In tender whispers, the bond is drawn.
In soft caresses, we find our peace,
Through endless emotion, our souls release.

Mapping stars upon night's expanse,
With every moment, we seize the chance.
Together we soar, no fear to show,
In this journey, endlessly we grow.

The echo of laughter, the sigh of dreams,
In the tapestry of life, love redeems.
A journey of hearts, forever in motion,
Together we stand, in endless emotion.

The Heart's Enigmatic Voyage

In whispers soft, the currents sway,
A sailor lost, come what may.
Stars above, like dreams in flight,
Guide the heart through endless night.

Each wave that crashes, secrets shared,
A voyage deep, so few have dared.
With every pulse, a compass true,
Navigating love, both tried and new.

The tempest brews, emotions clash,
Yet through the storm, we find the flash.
A beacon bright, our hearts align,
In turbulent seas, your hand in mine.

With every breath, horizons call,
In depths of love, we rise and fall.
Together strong, we chart the course,
Through heart's enigmas, love's great force.

Mirrored Reflections of Love's Puzzle

In silent rooms, your gaze reflects,
A thousand dreams, our hearts connect.
Through shards of glass, our visions blend,
In every corner, love transcends.

With every glance, the pieces shift,
A puzzle formed from love's sweet gift.
Together crafting, day by day,
What once was scattered finds its way.

The laughter shared, the tearful sighs,
In mirrored truths, no disguise lies.
The beauty found in every flaw,
Defines the love that we both draw.

In twilight's glow, reflections shine,
A tapestry of yours and mine.
In every heartbeat, we discover
The masterpiece that is our love.

Circles of Time and Tenderness

In circles drawn upon the sand,
We trace the moments, hand in hand.
Time weaves stories, rich and deep,
In gentle whispers, memories keep.

The sun will rise, the moon will wane,
In every joy, in every pain.
Tender glances cast like spells,
In circles where our magic dwells.

With laughter ringing, hearts unfold,
The warmth of love, a sight to behold.
Through seasons change, we stand as one,
In time's embrace, our lives well spun.

With rhythms soft, we dance through years,
In every smile, we conquer fears.
Together spinning, round and round,
In circles of love, we are unbound.

The Endless Spiral of Emotion

In spirals drawn, our feelings sway,
A dance of souls, come what may.
Each twist and turn, a pathway found,
In endless loops, our love is bound.

Through highs and lows, we intertwine,
In every step, your heart is mine.
The echoes call, a sweet refrain,
In spirals deep, love knows no pain.

With every heartbeat, spirals grow,
A constant flow, a gentle glow.
Our lives enclosed in this embrace,
A wondrous trip through time and space.

In endless spirals, we shall roam,
In every glance, we've found our home.
Together moving, wild and free,
The spiral of love, you and me.

A Dance in the Maze of Sentiments

In shadows deep, emotions play,
Whispers of joy, tinged with dismay.
Love's tender touch, a fleeting glance,
Hearts intertwine in a delicate dance.

Through corridors of longing we roam,
Searching for solace, a place called home.
Each turn reveals the truth we seek,
In the silence, our souls softly speak.

Yet doubt creeps in, a shadowy guest,
Testing our hearts, putting love to the test.
Still, we twirl in this labyrinth of fate,
Finding our way, it's never too late.

With every step, a lesson learned,
For in this maze, bright fires burn.
The pathways twist, the walls embrace,
In this intricate dance, we find our place.

So let us sway, hand in hand tight,
Navigating through day and night.
For love is a maze, complex yet true,
In the rhythm of feelings, it starts anew.

Constellations of Intricate Connections

Stars align in the velvet night,
Hidden stories in their light.
Each twinkle whispers of chance,
Galaxies converge in a cosmic dance.

We reach across the vast unknown,
Building bridges in a world of our own.
Threads of fate weave in and out,
In every heartbeat, we feel the doubt.

Yet in this chaos, a pattern unfolds,
Tales of friendship and love retold.
The universe smiles, bright and wide,
In the constellations, with us they bide.

Every bond, a star yet to shine,
Interlocking destinies, you are mine.
Through the vastness, we find our way,
Map of our hearts, guiding each day.

So let us gaze at the midnight skies,
In every twinkling light, a new surprise.
For in this realm of intricate ties,
The universe speaks as our spirit flies.

The Enigma of Wistful Sighs

In the stillness, a sigh escapes,
Memory's echo in quiet shapes.
Nostalgia lingers, a haunting tune,
Whispers of dreams beneath the moon.

We walk through shadows of what has been,
Chasing reflections, lost in between.
The heart remembers, though time may pass,
In the twilight, moments like glass.

Yet within each sigh, a story unfolds,
A tapestry woven with threads of gold.
Grief and joy, a delicate dance,
In whispered breaths, we find our chance.

The enigma lies in the space we hold,
A treasure of feelings, a sight to behold.
So let us breathe in the air of the night,
For within our sighs lies unexpected light.

In quiet corners of our hearts,
The echoes of love never truly departs.
For each wistful sigh sings a sweet refrain,
A melody soft in the embrace of pain.

Through the Garden of Eternal Possibility

In a garden lush with dreams untold,
Petals whisper secrets, both brave and bold.
Each bloom a symbol of what could be,
Filling the air with sweet possibility.

The paths we wander are lined with grace,
Explorations of passion in every space.
Sunlight dances on petals so fair,
Inviting the heart to pause and stare.

Yet amidst the beauty, uncertainties lie,
Clouds of doubt drift slowly by.
We gather courage, watered by tears,
Nurtured by hopes cultivated through years.

So let us wander, hand in hand,
Through this magical, enchanted land.
For within this garden, promise resides,
A sanctuary built where love abides.

In every seed, a story wakes,
A chance to blossom, new life it makes.
Through the garden where dreams intertwine,
Eternal possibilities, forever divine.